50 Chargrilled Recipes for the Home

By: Kelly Johnson

Table of Contents

- Chargrilled Ribeye Steak
- Chargrilled Chicken Breast with Lemon and Thyme
- Chargrilled Shrimp Skewers
- Chargrilled Portobello Mushrooms
- Chargrilled Lamb Chops with Mint
- Chargrilled Veggie Skewers
- Chargrilled Salmon with Dill Sauce
- Chargrilled Asparagus with Garlic Butter
- Chargrilled Hot Wings with Spicy Sauce
- Chargrilled Corn on the Cob with Herb Butter
- Chargrilled Tuna Steaks with Soy Glaze
- Chargrilled Pork Chops with Apple Salsa
- Chargrilled Garlic Butter Scallops
- Chargrilled Pineapple with Honey Glaze
- Chargrilled Tofu Steaks with Soy Marinade
- Chargrilled Sweet Potatoes with Chili
- Chargrilled Vegetables with Balsamic Glaze

- Chargrilled Beef Kebabs
- Chargrilled Swordfish with Lemon Zest
- Chargrilled Zucchini with Parmesan
- Chargrilled Chicken Thighs with Paprika
- Chargrilled Beef Tenderloin with Garlic
- Chargrilled Cauliflower Steaks
- Chargrilled Ratatouille
- Chargrilled Bacon-Wrapped Shrimp
- Chargrilled Eggplant with Tahini Sauce
- Chargrilled Flatbread with Herbs
- Chargrilled Duck Breast with Orange Glaze
- Chargrilled Char Siu Pork
- Chargrilled Fajita Chicken
- Chargrilled Avocados with Lime
- Chargrilled Marinated Vegetables
- Chargrilled Tomatoes with Basil
- Chargrilled Mahi-Mahi with Mango Salsa
- Chargrilled Skirt Steak with Chimichurri
- Chargrilled Sweet Peppers with Goat Cheese

- Chargrilled Octopus with Garlic and Lemon
- Chargrilled Beef Short Ribs
- Chargrilled Prawns with Lemon and Garlic
- Chargrilled Salmon with Avocado Salsa
- Chargrilled Artichokes with Lemon
- Chargrilled Brie with Jam
- Chargrilled Balsamic Mushrooms
- Chargrilled Chicken with Pesto
- Chargrilled Fennel with Lemon
- Chargrilled Fish Tacos with Cabbage Slaw
- Chargrilled Skewered Pork with Pineapple
- Chargrilled Broccoli with Parmesan
- Chargrilled Pears with Blue Cheese
- Chargrilled Garlic and Herb Lamb Ribs

Chargrilled Ribeye Steak

Ingredients:

- 2 ribeye steaks (about 1.5 inches thick)
- 2 tablespoons olive oil
- 2 teaspoons garlic powder
- 1 teaspoon rosemary, chopped
- Salt and pepper to taste

Instructions:

1. Preheat grill to high heat.
2. Rub the ribeye steaks with olive oil, garlic powder, rosemary, salt, and pepper.
3. Grill steaks for 4–6 minutes per side for medium-rare, or longer for your preferred doneness.
4. Let steaks rest for 5–10 minutes before slicing.
5. Serve with a side of roasted vegetables or your favorite sauce.

Chargrilled Chicken Breast with Lemon and Thyme

Ingredients:

- 2 boneless, skinless chicken breasts
- 2 tablespoons olive oil
- 1 lemon, zested and juiced
- 1 tablespoon fresh thyme, chopped
- Salt and pepper to taste

Instructions:

1. Preheat grill to medium-high heat.
2. Mix olive oil, lemon zest, lemon juice, thyme, salt, and pepper in a bowl.
3. Coat chicken breasts in the marinade and let rest for 15 minutes.
4. Grill chicken for 6–8 minutes per side, until cooked through and the internal temperature reaches 165°F (74°C).
5. Serve with a fresh salad or grilled vegetables.

Chargrilled Shrimp Skewers

Ingredients:

- 12 large shrimp, peeled and deveined
- 2 tablespoons olive oil
- 2 tablespoons lemon juice
- 1 teaspoon smoked paprika
- 1 clove garlic, minced
- Salt and pepper to taste

Instructions:

1. Preheat grill to medium-high heat.
2. In a bowl, mix olive oil, lemon juice, smoked paprika, garlic, salt, and pepper.
3. Toss shrimp in the marinade and thread onto skewers.
4. Grill shrimp for 2–3 minutes per side, until pink and opaque.
5. Serve with a squeeze of fresh lemon juice and a side of rice or salad.

Chargrilled Portobello Mushrooms
Ingredients:

- 4 large Portobello mushrooms, stems removed
- 2 tablespoons olive oil
- 2 teaspoons balsamic vinegar
- 1 clove garlic, minced
- Salt and pepper to taste

Instructions:

1. Preheat grill to medium heat.
2. Mix olive oil, balsamic vinegar, garlic, salt, and pepper in a bowl.
3. Brush the mushrooms with the marinade and let sit for 10 minutes.
4. Grill mushrooms for 4–5 minutes per side, until tender and lightly charred.
5. Serve as a vegetarian main dish or as a side to grilled meats.

Chargrilled Lamb Chops with Mint

Ingredients:

- 4 lamb chops
- 2 tablespoons olive oil
- 1 tablespoon fresh mint, chopped
- 2 teaspoons garlic powder
- Salt and pepper to taste

Instructions:

1. Preheat grill to medium-high heat.
2. Rub lamb chops with olive oil, mint, garlic powder, salt, and pepper.
3. Grill lamb chops for 4–5 minutes per side, or until desired doneness is reached (medium-rare is ideal).
4. Let rest for 5 minutes before serving.
5. Serve with a fresh mint yogurt sauce or alongside roasted potatoes.

Chargrilled Veggie Skewers
Ingredients:

- 1 red bell pepper, chopped
- 1 zucchini, sliced
- 1 red onion, chopped
- 1 cup cherry tomatoes
- 2 tablespoons olive oil
- 1 teaspoon oregano
- Salt and pepper to taste

Instructions:

1. Preheat grill to medium heat.
2. Thread vegetables onto skewers, alternating between them.
3. Brush with olive oil, oregano, salt, and pepper.
4. Grill veggie skewers for 3–5 minutes per side, until charred and tender.
5. Serve with a drizzle of balsamic glaze or a side of couscous.

Chargrilled Salmon with Dill Sauce
Ingredients:

- 2 salmon fillets
- 2 tablespoons olive oil
- Salt and pepper to taste
- 1/2 cup Greek yogurt
- 1 tablespoon fresh dill, chopped
- 1 tablespoon lemon juice

Instructions:

1. Preheat grill to medium-high heat.
2. Rub salmon fillets with olive oil, salt, and pepper.
3. Grill salmon for 4–5 minutes per side, until the fish flakes easily with a fork.
4. In a bowl, mix Greek yogurt, dill, and lemon juice to make the dill sauce.
5. Serve grilled salmon with a generous spoonful of dill sauce on top.

Chargrilled Asparagus with Garlic Butter

Ingredients:

- 1 bunch asparagus, trimmed
- 2 tablespoons olive oil
- 2 tablespoons butter, melted
- 2 cloves garlic, minced
- Salt and pepper to taste

Instructions:

1. Preheat grill to medium heat.
2. Toss asparagus with olive oil, salt, and pepper.
3. Grill asparagus for 3–5 minutes, turning occasionally, until tender and charred.
4. In a small bowl, mix melted butter with garlic.
5. Drizzle garlic butter over grilled asparagus and serve.

Chargrilled Hot Wings with Spicy Sauce

Ingredients:

- 12 chicken wings
- 2 tablespoons olive oil
- Salt and pepper to taste
- 1/2 cup hot sauce
- 2 tablespoons honey
- 1 tablespoon apple cider vinegar

Instructions:

1. Preheat grill to medium-high heat.
2. Toss wings with olive oil, salt, and pepper.
3. Grill wings for 8–10 minutes per side, until crispy and cooked through.
4. In a small bowl, mix hot sauce, honey, and vinegar.
5. Toss the grilled wings in the spicy sauce and serve immediately.

Chargrilled Corn on the Cob with Herb Butter

Ingredients:

- 4 ears of corn, husked
- 4 tablespoons unsalted butter, softened
- 1 tablespoon fresh parsley, chopped
- 1 tablespoon fresh chives, chopped
- 1 teaspoon garlic powder
- Salt and pepper to taste

Instructions:

1. Preheat grill to medium heat.
2. Grill corn on the cob for 10–12 minutes, turning occasionally until charred and tender.
3. In a small bowl, mix softened butter with parsley, chives, garlic powder, salt, and pepper.
4. Once the corn is grilled, spread the herb butter over the warm cobs.
5. Serve immediately with a sprinkle of extra herbs if desired.

Chargrilled Tuna Steaks with Soy Glaze

Ingredients:

- 2 tuna steaks (about 1 inch thick)
- 2 tablespoons soy sauce
- 1 tablespoon honey
- 1 teaspoon sesame oil
- 1 clove garlic, minced
- Salt and pepper to taste

Instructions:

1. Preheat grill to medium-high heat.
2. In a bowl, whisk together soy sauce, honey, sesame oil, garlic, salt, and pepper.
3. Brush the tuna steaks with the marinade and let them sit for 10–15 minutes.
4. Grill tuna steaks for 3–4 minutes per side for rare to medium-rare, or longer if desired.
5. Serve the tuna steaks with a drizzle of extra soy glaze and a sprinkle of sesame seeds.

Chargrilled Pork Chops with Apple Salsa

Ingredients:

- 4 bone-in pork chops
- 2 tablespoons olive oil
- 1 teaspoon paprika
- Salt and pepper to taste
- 2 apples, peeled and diced
- 1/2 red onion, diced
- 1 tablespoon fresh cilantro, chopped
- 1 tablespoon lime juice

Instructions:

1. Preheat grill to medium-high heat.
2. Rub pork chops with olive oil, paprika, salt, and pepper.
3. Grill pork chops for 6–8 minutes per side until the internal temperature reaches 145°F (63°C).
4. While the chops are grilling, mix diced apples, red onion, cilantro, and lime juice in a bowl to make the apple salsa.
5. Serve the grilled pork chops topped with fresh apple salsa.

Chargrilled Garlic Butter Scallops
Ingredients:

- 12 large scallops, cleaned and patted dry
- 2 tablespoons olive oil
- 2 tablespoons unsalted butter, melted
- 2 cloves garlic, minced
- 1 tablespoon fresh lemon juice
- Salt and pepper to taste

Instructions:

1. Preheat grill to medium-high heat.
2. Brush the scallops with olive oil and season with salt and pepper.
3. Grill scallops for 2–3 minutes per side until lightly charred and opaque.
4. While grilling, mix melted butter, garlic, and lemon juice.
5. Drizzle garlic butter over the grilled scallops and serve immediately.

Chargrilled Pineapple with Honey Glaze

Ingredients:

- 1 ripe pineapple, peeled and sliced into rings
- 2 tablespoons honey
- 1 tablespoon lime juice
- 1/2 teaspoon cinnamon

Instructions:

1. Preheat grill to medium heat.
2. Mix honey, lime juice, and cinnamon in a small bowl.
3. Brush pineapple rings with the honey glaze.
4. Grill pineapple for 2–3 minutes per side, until caramelized and slightly charred.
5. Serve as a sweet side or dessert, drizzled with extra glaze.

Chargrilled Tofu Steaks with Soy Marinade

Ingredients:

- 1 block firm tofu, pressed and sliced into 1-inch thick steaks
- 2 tablespoons soy sauce
- 1 tablespoon sesame oil
- 1 teaspoon rice vinegar
- 1 teaspoon maple syrup
- 1 teaspoon grated ginger
- 1 clove garlic, minced

Instructions:

1. Preheat grill to medium heat.
2. Whisk together soy sauce, sesame oil, rice vinegar, maple syrup, ginger, and garlic in a bowl.
3. Marinate tofu steaks in the mixture for 15–20 minutes.
4. Grill tofu for 3–4 minutes per side until crispy and golden brown.
5. Serve the tofu steaks with a sprinkle of sesame seeds or a drizzle of extra soy sauce.

Chargrilled Sweet Potatoes with Chili

Ingredients:

- 2 large sweet potatoes, sliced into 1/2-inch rounds
- 2 tablespoons olive oil
- 1 teaspoon chili powder
- 1/2 teaspoon cumin
- Salt and pepper to taste
- 1 tablespoon fresh cilantro, chopped

Instructions:

1. Preheat grill to medium heat.
2. Toss sweet potato slices with olive oil, chili powder, cumin, salt, and pepper.
3. Grill sweet potatoes for 4–5 minutes per side, until tender and charred.
4. Garnish with fresh cilantro and serve.

Chargrilled Vegetables with Balsamic Glaze

Ingredients:

- 1 red bell pepper, sliced
- 1 zucchini, sliced
- 1 yellow squash, sliced
- 1 red onion, sliced
- 2 tablespoons olive oil
- Salt and pepper to taste
- 1/4 cup balsamic glaze

Instructions:

1. Preheat grill to medium heat.
2. Toss vegetables with olive oil, salt, and pepper.
3. Grill vegetables for 3–5 minutes per side, until tender and lightly charred.
4. Drizzle with balsamic glaze and serve as a colorful side dish.

Chargrilled Beef Kebabs

Ingredients:

- 1 lb beef sirloin, cut into 1-inch cubes
- 1 red bell pepper, cut into chunks
- 1 onion, cut into chunks
- 1 zucchini, sliced
- 2 tablespoons olive oil
- 2 tablespoons soy sauce
- 1 tablespoon lemon juice
- 1 teaspoon cumin
- 1 teaspoon paprika
- Salt and pepper to taste

Instructions:

1. Preheat grill to medium-high heat.
2. In a bowl, mix olive oil, soy sauce, lemon juice, cumin, paprika, salt, and pepper.
3. Thread beef, bell pepper, onion, and zucchini onto skewers.
4. Brush with marinade and grill for 8–10 minutes, turning occasionally until beef is cooked to desired doneness.
5. Serve with a side of rice or couscous.

Chargrilled Swordfish with Lemon Zest

Ingredients:

- 2 swordfish steaks
- 2 tablespoons olive oil
- Zest of 1 lemon
- 1 tablespoon fresh parsley, chopped
- Salt and pepper to taste

Instructions:

1. Preheat grill to medium-high heat.
2. Rub swordfish steaks with olive oil, lemon zest, salt, and pepper.
3. Grill swordfish for 3–4 minutes per side, until the fish flakes easily with a fork.
4. Garnish with chopped parsley and serve with grilled vegetables or a salad.

Chargrilled Zucchini with Parmesan

Ingredients:

- 2 zucchinis, sliced into rounds
- 2 tablespoons olive oil
- 1 teaspoon garlic powder
- Salt and pepper to taste
- 1/4 cup grated Parmesan cheese

Instructions:

1. Preheat grill to medium heat.
2. Toss zucchini slices with olive oil, garlic powder, salt, and pepper.
3. Grill zucchini for 2–3 minutes per side, until tender and lightly charred.
4. Sprinkle with Parmesan cheese and serve as a side dish.

Chargrilled Chicken Thighs with Paprika
Ingredients:

- 4 bone-in chicken thighs
- 2 tablespoons olive oil
- 1 tablespoon paprika
- 1 teaspoon garlic powder
- Salt and pepper to taste

Instructions:

1. Preheat grill to medium-high heat.
2. Rub chicken thighs with olive oil, paprika, garlic powder, salt, and pepper.
3. Grill chicken for 6–8 minutes per side, until the internal temperature reaches 165°F (74°C).
4. Serve with grilled vegetables or a fresh salad.

Chargrilled Beef Tenderloin with Garlic

Ingredients:

- 2 beef tenderloin steaks (about 1 inch thick)
- 2 tablespoons olive oil
- 2 cloves garlic, minced
- 1 teaspoon rosemary, chopped
- Salt and pepper to taste

Instructions:

1. Preheat grill to medium-high heat.
2. Rub the steaks with olive oil, garlic, rosemary, salt, and pepper.
3. Grill tenderloin for 4–5 minutes per side for medium-rare, or longer for your desired doneness.
4. Let rest for 5 minutes before serving with your favorite sides.

Chargrilled Cauliflower Steaks

Ingredients:

- 1 head cauliflower, cut into thick slices
- 2 tablespoons olive oil
- 1 teaspoon garlic powder
- 1 teaspoon paprika
- Salt and pepper to taste

Instructions:

1. Preheat grill to medium heat.
2. Brush cauliflower steaks with olive oil and sprinkle with garlic powder, paprika, salt, and pepper.
3. Grill cauliflower for 3–4 minutes per side, until golden and tender.
4. Serve with a squeeze of lemon juice or a drizzle of tahini.

Chargrilled Ratatouille

Ingredients:

- 1 eggplant, sliced
- 1 zucchini, sliced
- 1 red bell pepper, sliced
- 1 yellow bell pepper, sliced
- 1 onion, sliced
- 2 tablespoons olive oil
- 1 teaspoon dried thyme
- Salt and pepper to taste

Instructions:

1. Preheat grill to medium heat.
2. Toss the vegetables in olive oil, thyme, salt, and pepper.
3. Grill the vegetables for 3–4 minutes per side, until charred and tender.
4. Serve as a side dish or over couscous or quinoa for a hearty meal.

Chargrilled Bacon-Wrapped Shrimp

Ingredients:

- 12 large shrimp, peeled and deveined
- 6 slices bacon, cut in half
- 1 tablespoon olive oil
- 1 teaspoon paprika
- Salt and pepper to taste

Instructions:

1. Preheat grill to medium-high heat.
2. Wrap each shrimp with a half slice of bacon and secure with toothpicks.
3. Brush with olive oil and season with paprika, salt, and pepper.
4. Grill shrimp for 2–3 minutes per side, until bacon is crispy and shrimp is cooked through.
5. Serve with a squeeze of lemon.

Chargrilled Eggplant with Tahini Sauce

Ingredients:

- 2 eggplants, sliced into 1-inch thick rounds
- 2 tablespoons olive oil
- Salt and pepper to taste
- 1/4 cup tahini
- 1 tablespoon lemon juice
- 1 tablespoon olive oil

Instructions:

1. Preheat grill to medium heat.
2. Brush eggplant slices with olive oil, salt, and pepper.
3. Grill eggplant for 3–4 minutes per side, until tender and charred.
4. In a small bowl, whisk tahini, lemon juice, and olive oil.
5. Drizzle tahini sauce over the grilled eggplant and serve with fresh herbs.

Chargrilled Flatbread with Herbs

Ingredients:

- 2 flatbreads
- 2 tablespoons olive oil
- 1 tablespoon fresh rosemary, chopped
- 1 tablespoon fresh thyme, chopped
- Salt to taste

Instructions:

1. Preheat grill to medium-high heat.
2. Brush flatbreads with olive oil and sprinkle with rosemary, thyme, and salt.
3. Grill flatbreads for 2–3 minutes per side, until golden and crispy.
4. Serve warm as an appetizer or with a dip of your choice.

Chargrilled Duck Breast with Orange Glaze
Ingredients:

- 2 duck breasts
- 2 tablespoons olive oil
- Salt and pepper to taste
- 1/2 cup orange juice
- 2 tablespoons honey
- 1 tablespoon soy sauce
- 1 teaspoon fresh thyme

Instructions:

1. Preheat grill to medium-high heat.
2. Score the skin of the duck breasts and rub with olive oil, salt, and pepper.
3. Grill the duck breasts skin-side down for 6–8 minutes, then flip and grill for another 4–5 minutes for medium-rare or until your desired doneness.
4. While the duck grills, in a saucepan, combine orange juice, honey, soy sauce, and thyme. Simmer over medium heat until it thickens into a glaze.
5. Drizzle the orange glaze over the grilled duck breasts and serve.

Chargrilled Char Siu Pork
Ingredients:

- 1 lb pork tenderloin
- 1/4 cup hoisin sauce
- 1/4 cup soy sauce
- 2 tablespoons honey
- 1 tablespoon Chinese five-spice powder
- 2 cloves garlic, minced
- 1 tablespoon rice vinegar
- 1 tablespoon sesame oil

Instructions:

1. Preheat grill to medium-high heat.
2. Mix hoisin sauce, soy sauce, honey, five-spice powder, garlic, rice vinegar, and sesame oil in a bowl.
3. Marinate the pork tenderloin in the sauce for at least 1 hour.
4. Grill the pork for 6–8 minutes per side, basting with the marinade as it cooks.
5. Once the pork reaches an internal temperature of 145°F (63°C), let it rest before slicing and serving.

Chargrilled Fajita Chicken

Ingredients:

- 4 boneless, skinless chicken breasts
- 2 tablespoons olive oil
- 1 tablespoon lime juice
- 1 tablespoon chili powder
- 1 teaspoon cumin
- 1 teaspoon paprika
- Salt and pepper to taste

Instructions:

1. Preheat grill to medium-high heat.
2. In a bowl, mix olive oil, lime juice, chili powder, cumin, paprika, salt, and pepper.
3. Coat the chicken breasts with the marinade and let sit for 15–30 minutes.
4. Grill the chicken for 5–7 minutes per side, until the internal temperature reaches 165°F (74°C).
5. Serve the fajita chicken with tortillas, sautéed peppers, and onions.

Chargrilled Avocados with Lime

Ingredients:

- 2 ripe avocados, halved and pitted
- 1 tablespoon olive oil
- Salt and pepper to taste
- 1 lime, cut into wedges

Instructions:

1. Preheat grill to medium heat.
2. Brush the avocado halves with olive oil and season with salt and pepper.
3. Grill the avocados flesh-side down for 3–4 minutes until grill marks appear.
4. Squeeze fresh lime juice over the grilled avocados and serve as a side or appetizer.

Chargrilled Marinated Vegetables
Ingredients:

- 1 red bell pepper, cut into chunks
- 1 zucchini, sliced
- 1 red onion, cut into wedges
- 1 eggplant, sliced
- 2 tablespoons olive oil
- 1 tablespoon balsamic vinegar
- 1 teaspoon dried oregano
- Salt and pepper to taste

Instructions:

1. Preheat grill to medium heat.
2. Toss the vegetables with olive oil, balsamic vinegar, oregano, salt, and pepper.
3. Grill the vegetables for 3–4 minutes per side until tender and slightly charred.
4. Serve with a drizzle of balsamic glaze for extra flavor.

Chargrilled Tomatoes with Basil
Ingredients:

- 4 large tomatoes, halved
- 2 tablespoons olive oil
- 1 tablespoon balsamic vinegar
- 1 teaspoon dried oregano
- Salt and pepper to taste
- Fresh basil leaves for garnish

Instructions:

1. Preheat grill to medium heat.
2. Brush tomato halves with olive oil, balsamic vinegar, oregano, salt, and pepper.
3. Grill tomatoes flesh-side down for 3–4 minutes, until grill marks form and the tomatoes are tender.
4. Garnish with fresh basil leaves and serve as a side or topping for grilled meats.

Chargrilled Mahi-Mahi with Mango Salsa

Ingredients:

- 2 mahi-mahi fillets
- 1 tablespoon olive oil
- Salt and pepper to taste
- 1 mango, diced
- 1/4 red onion, finely diced
- 1 tablespoon cilantro, chopped
- 1 tablespoon lime juice

Instructions:

1. Preheat grill to medium-high heat.
2. Brush mahi-mahi fillets with olive oil and season with salt and pepper.
3. Grill the fish for 4–5 minutes per side, until it flakes easily with a fork.
4. While the fish grills, combine mango, red onion, cilantro, and lime juice in a bowl to make the salsa.
5. Serve the grilled mahi-mahi topped with fresh mango salsa.

Chargrilled Skirt Steak with Chimichurri

Ingredients:

- 1 lb skirt steak
- 2 tablespoons olive oil
- Salt and pepper to taste
- 1/4 cup parsley, chopped
- 2 tablespoons red wine vinegar
- 2 tablespoons olive oil
- 2 cloves garlic, minced
- 1/2 teaspoon red pepper flakes

Instructions:

1. Preheat grill to medium-high heat.
2. Rub the skirt steak with olive oil, salt, and pepper.
3. Grill the steak for 3–4 minutes per side, until it reaches your desired doneness.
4. In a bowl, combine parsley, red wine vinegar, olive oil, garlic, and red pepper flakes to make the chimichurri.
5. Slice the steak against the grain and serve with chimichurri on top.

Chargrilled Sweet Peppers with Goat Cheese

Ingredients:

- 4 sweet peppers (red, yellow, or orange)
- 2 tablespoons olive oil
- Salt and pepper to taste
- 1/2 cup goat cheese, crumbled
- 1 tablespoon fresh basil, chopped

Instructions:

1. Preheat grill to medium heat.
2. Brush the sweet peppers with olive oil and season with salt and pepper.
3. Grill the peppers for 5–6 minutes, turning occasionally, until they are tender and charred.
4. Once grilled, cut the peppers open and remove the seeds.
5. Fill the peppers with goat cheese and garnish with fresh basil.

Chargrilled Octopus with Garlic and Lemon
Ingredients:

- 2 octopus tentacles (pre-cooked or fresh)
- 2 tablespoons olive oil
- 2 cloves garlic, minced
- Juice of 1 lemon
- 1 teaspoon smoked paprika
- Salt and pepper to taste
- Fresh parsley, chopped (for garnish)

Instructions:

1. Preheat grill to medium-high heat.
2. Rub the octopus tentacles with olive oil, garlic, lemon juice, smoked paprika, salt, and pepper.
3. Grill octopus for 3–4 minutes per side, until crispy and charred.
4. Garnish with fresh parsley and serve with a side of grilled vegetables or a salad.

Chargrilled Beef Short Ribs

Ingredients:

- 2 lbs beef short ribs
- 3 tablespoons soy sauce
- 1 tablespoon brown sugar
- 2 cloves garlic, minced
- 1 tablespoon ginger, grated
- 1 tablespoon sesame oil
- Salt and pepper to taste

Instructions:

1. Preheat grill to medium-high heat.
2. In a bowl, whisk together soy sauce, brown sugar, garlic, ginger, sesame oil, salt, and pepper.
3. Marinate the short ribs in the mixture for 1–2 hours.
4. Grill the ribs for 6–8 minutes per side, until tender and caramelized.
5. Serve with steamed rice or grilled vegetables.

Chargrilled Prawns with Lemon and Garlic

Ingredients:

- 12 large prawns, peeled and deveined
- 2 tablespoons olive oil
- 2 cloves garlic, minced
- Zest and juice of 1 lemon
- Salt and pepper to taste
- Fresh parsley for garnish

Instructions:

1. Preheat grill to medium-high heat.
2. Toss the prawns in olive oil, garlic, lemon zest, lemon juice, salt, and pepper.
3. Grill prawns for 2–3 minutes per side, until they turn pink and are cooked through.
4. Garnish with fresh parsley and serve with a side of grilled vegetables or a fresh salad.

Chargrilled Salmon with Avocado Salsa

Ingredients:

- 2 salmon fillets
- 1 tablespoon olive oil
- Salt and pepper to taste
- 1 avocado, diced
- 1/4 red onion, finely chopped
- 1 tablespoon cilantro, chopped
- 1 tablespoon lime juice

Instructions:

1. Preheat grill to medium-high heat.
2. Brush the salmon fillets with olive oil and season with salt and pepper.
3. Grill the salmon for 4–5 minutes per side, until the fish flakes easily with a fork.
4. While the salmon grills, combine avocado, red onion, cilantro, and lime juice in a bowl to make the salsa.
5. Serve the grilled salmon topped with the avocado salsa.

Chargrilled Artichokes with Lemon

Ingredients:

- 4 fresh artichokes
- 2 tablespoons olive oil
- 1 lemon, halved
- Salt and pepper to taste
- 2 cloves garlic, minced

Instructions:

1. Preheat grill to medium-high heat.
2. Trim the artichokes, cutting off the tops and removing the outer leaves.
3. Boil the artichokes for 10–15 minutes until tender, then drain and let cool slightly.
4. Cut the artichokes in half and brush with olive oil, lemon juice, garlic, salt, and pepper.
5. Grill the artichokes for 4–5 minutes per side until lightly charred and crispy.
6. Serve with extra lemon wedges for squeezing.

Chargrilled Brie with Jam

Ingredients:

- 1 wheel of brie cheese
- 2 tablespoons olive oil
- 2 tablespoons fruit jam (fig, raspberry, or apricot work well)
- Fresh thyme or rosemary for garnish

Instructions:

1. Preheat grill to medium heat.
2. Brush the brie wheel with olive oil and place it on a piece of foil or a grilling tray.
3. Grill the brie for 4–5 minutes until the outside is golden and soft inside.
4. Drizzle the jam over the grilled brie and garnish with fresh thyme or rosemary.
5. Serve with crusty bread or crackers for dipping.

Chargrilled Balsamic Mushrooms

Ingredients:

- 12 large button mushrooms, cleaned and stems removed
- 2 tablespoons balsamic vinegar
- 2 tablespoons olive oil
- 1 teaspoon garlic powder
- Salt and pepper to taste

Instructions:

1. Preheat grill to medium heat.
2. Toss the mushrooms with balsamic vinegar, olive oil, garlic powder, salt, and pepper.
3. Grill the mushrooms for 3–4 minutes per side, until tender and caramelized.
4. Serve as a side dish or as a topping for grilled meats.

Chargrilled Chicken with Pesto

Ingredients:

- 4 boneless, skinless chicken breasts
- 2 tablespoons olive oil
- Salt and pepper to taste
- 1/2 cup pesto sauce (store-bought or homemade)

Instructions:

1. Preheat grill to medium-high heat.
2. Brush chicken breasts with olive oil and season with salt and pepper.
3. Grill chicken for 5–6 minutes per side, until the internal temperature reaches 165°F (74°C).
4. Brush the grilled chicken with pesto sauce before serving.
5. Serve with a side of grilled vegetables or a fresh salad.

Chargrilled Fennel with Lemon

Ingredients:

- 2 fennel bulbs, trimmed and sliced into wedges
- 2 tablespoons olive oil
- Salt and pepper to taste
- Zest and juice of 1 lemon
- Fresh dill, chopped (optional)

Instructions:

1. Preheat grill to medium heat.
2. Toss fennel wedges with olive oil, salt, and pepper.
3. Grill the fennel for 3–4 minutes per side until tender and slightly charred.
4. Drizzle with lemon juice and zest, and garnish with fresh dill if desired.
5. Serve as a flavorful side dish with grilled meats or fish.

Chargrilled Fish Tacos with Cabbage Slaw
Ingredients:

- 2 white fish fillets (e.g., tilapia, cod, or mahi-mahi)
- 1 tablespoon olive oil
- Salt and pepper to taste
- 1 teaspoon chili powder
- 8 small corn tortillas
- 1/2 small red cabbage, shredded
- 1/4 cup cilantro, chopped
- 2 tablespoons lime juice
- 1/4 cup sour cream

Instructions:

1. Preheat grill to medium-high heat.
2. Brush the fish fillets with olive oil, then season with salt, pepper, and chili powder.
3. Grill the fish for 3–4 minutes per side until flaky and cooked through.
4. In a bowl, toss together the shredded cabbage, cilantro, lime juice, and a pinch of salt.
5. Grill the corn tortillas for about 30 seconds per side until warmed through and slightly charred.
6. Assemble tacos by placing the grilled fish on tortillas, topping with cabbage slaw, and drizzling with sour cream.

7. Serve with extra lime wedges.

Chargrilled Skewered Pork with Pineapple

Ingredients:

- 1 lb pork tenderloin, cut into cubes
- 1/2 pineapple, peeled and cut into chunks
- 2 tablespoons soy sauce
- 1 tablespoon honey
- 1 tablespoon olive oil
- 1 clove garlic, minced
- 1 teaspoon ginger, grated
- Salt and pepper to taste

Instructions:

1. Preheat grill to medium-high heat.
2. In a bowl, combine soy sauce, honey, olive oil, garlic, ginger, salt, and pepper.
3. Thread the pork cubes and pineapple chunks onto skewers, alternating between pork and pineapple.
4. Brush with the marinade and grill for 4–5 minutes per side until the pork is cooked through and caramelized.
5. Serve the skewers with a side of rice or a fresh salad.

Chargrilled Broccoli with Parmesan

Ingredients:

- 2 heads of broccoli, cut into florets
- 2 tablespoons olive oil
- Salt and pepper to taste
- 1/4 cup grated Parmesan cheese
- 1 tablespoon lemon juice

Instructions:

1. Preheat grill to medium-high heat.
2. Toss broccoli florets with olive oil, salt, and pepper.
3. Grill the broccoli for 4–5 minutes, turning occasionally, until slightly charred and tender.
4. Remove from the grill and sprinkle with grated Parmesan cheese and a drizzle of lemon juice.
5. Serve as a side dish to grilled meats or seafood.

Chargrilled Pears with Blue Cheese

Ingredients:

- 4 ripe pears, halved and cored
- 2 tablespoons olive oil
- Salt and pepper to taste
- 1/4 cup crumbled blue cheese
- 1 tablespoon honey
- Fresh thyme for garnish

Instructions:

1. Preheat grill to medium heat.
2. Brush the pear halves with olive oil and season with salt and pepper.
3. Grill the pears cut-side down for 3–4 minutes until grill marks appear and they are slightly softened.
4. Remove from the grill, drizzle with honey, and top with crumbled blue cheese.
5. Garnish with fresh thyme and serve as an appetizer or side dish.

Chargrilled Garlic and Herb Lamb Ribs

Ingredients:

- 2 racks of lamb ribs
- 2 tablespoons olive oil
- 4 cloves garlic, minced
- 1 tablespoon fresh rosemary, chopped
- 1 tablespoon fresh thyme, chopped
- Salt and pepper to taste

Instructions:

1. Preheat grill to medium-high heat.
2. Rub the lamb ribs with olive oil, garlic, rosemary, thyme, salt, and pepper.
3. Grill the ribs for 5–7 minutes per side, or until the internal temperature reaches 145°F (63°C) for medium-rare.
4. Let the lamb rest for 5 minutes before slicing between the bones.
5. Serve with grilled vegetables or a fresh mint yogurt sauce.

www.ingramcontent.com/pod-product-compliance
Lightning Source LLC
LaVergne TN
LVHW061950070526
838199LV00060B/4059